WHAT TO EXPECT
WHEN YOU'RE
IMMIGRATING

FOR MARNIE/SARAH AND GRUMPY

WHAT TO EXPECT
WHEN YOU'RE
IMMIGRATING

N A S H

Affirm
press

ABOUT THE AUTHOR—ILLUSTRATOR

NASH IS A SRI LANKAN BORN MULTIDISCIPLINARY DESIGNER ARTIST BASED IN MELBOURNE, WHERE HE HAS LIVED SINCE 2012. HIS WORK IS BOTH CYNICAL SOCIAL COMMENTARY AND AN ACCOUNT OF HIS PERSONAL EXPERIENCE AS AN IMMIGRANT — THE 'OTHER' IN ANY SOCIETY. *WHAT TO EXPECT WHEN YOU'RE IMMIGRATING* IS HIS FIRST BOOK.

WHAT TO EXPECT...

MOST OF US KNOW WHAT IT'S LIKE TO MOVE HOUSE — TO PACK EVERYTHING YOU DEEM IMPORTANT AND LEAVE BEHIND THE PLACE YOU'VE KNOWN YOUR WHOLE LIFE. ALL THE BOXES FILLED WITH MEMORIES, BOTH GOOD AND BAD, LOADED ONTO THE TRUCK, READY TO GO.

YOU'RE NERVOUSLY EXCITED TO FACE THE CHALLENGES YOU WILL ENCOUNTER WHEN YOU REACH YOUR NEW HOME, WHICH HAS BEEN ADVERTISED AS MUCH BETTER THAN THE ONE YOU'RE LEAVING.

IMAGINE YOU ARRIVE AT THE NEW NEIGHBOURHOOD, WHERE EVERYTHING SEEMS NEW AND SHINY. BUT IT DOESN'T HAVE CHEAPER RENT AND THE ONLY INTERACTION YOU'VE HAD WITH YOUR NEIGHBOURS WASN'T A WELCOMING WAVE, BUT BEING BLATANTLY TOLD TO 'GO BACK' OVER YOUR SHARED FENCE.

TO MAKE THINGS WORSE, MOST OF YOUR OLD STUFF DOESN'T FIT INTO YOUR NEW PLACE. NOW YOU'VE GOT TO DECIDE WHAT YOU WANT TO KEEP, THROW AWAY OR SOMEHOW ADJUST TO FIT INTO THE PLACE.
FEELS A BIT OVERWHELMING, HUH?

NOW IMAGINE INSTEAD OF MOVING HOUSES AND NEIGHBOURHOODS, THAT YOU'VE MOVED TO A DIFFERENT COUNTRY, ON A NEW CONTINENT. THE OLD STUFF THAT YOU BROUGHT WITH YOU BUT COULDN'T FIT IN THE HOUSE ARE THE VIEWS AND BELIEFS YOU WERE BROUGHT UP ON THAT AREN'T COMPATIBLE WITH THE NEW SOCIETY YOU'RE IN.

AND THE NEIGHBOURS WHO ASKED YOU TO 'GO BACK'? WELL, UNFORTUNATELY THAT COULD ACTUALLY BE WHAT YOUR NEIGHBOURS ARE LIKE.

ALTHOUGH THE ISSUES FACED BY BOTH THE IMMIGRANT AND THE SOCIETY THEY MOVE INTO ARE MUCH BIGGER THAN ANY TWO INDIVIDUALS, I HOPE SHARING MY EXPERIENCES THROUGH HUMOROUS ILLUSTRATIONS WILL HELP YOU CRITICALLY ENGAGE WITH THE NARRATIVES SURROUNDING IMMIGRANTS AND REFUGEES.

WHAT TO EXPECT WHEN YOU'RE IMMIGRATING IS MY ATTEMPT AT SHARING THE UPS AND DOWNS OF THIS EXPERIENCE, THROUGH A COMPILATION OF TONGUE-IN-CHEEK ILLUSTRATIONS (IN NO PARTICULAR ORDER).

IT CAN BE READ BOTH AS A 'WHAT TO EXPECT' GUIDE FOR AN IMMIGRANT, OR HELP OTHERS EMPATHISE WITH THEIR SITUATION —
AND MAYBE EVEN SHARE A LAUGH TOGETHER!

NASH

PAPERWORK.

YOUR NAME IS NOT GONNA FIT IN THE BOXES. LOOK FORWARD TO A NICKNAME.

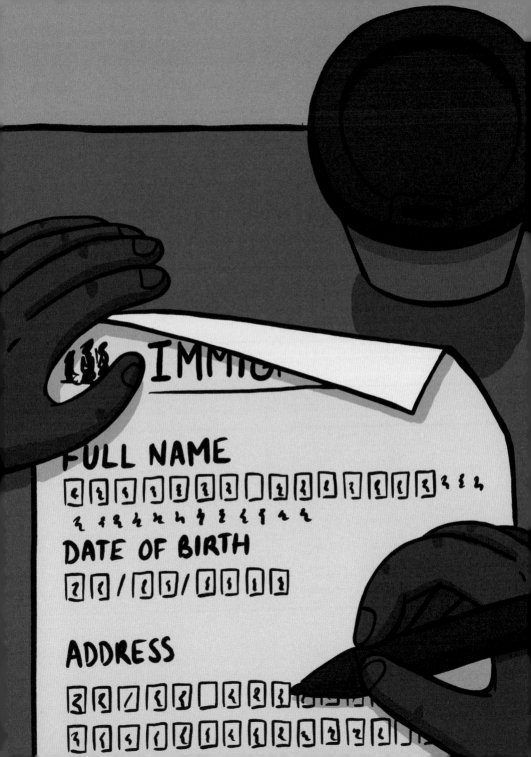

YOU WILL HAVE TO STAND IN A
LOT OF QUEUES.

COMPULSORY MEDICAL
CHECK-UPS MAY COST AN ARM
AND A LEG...

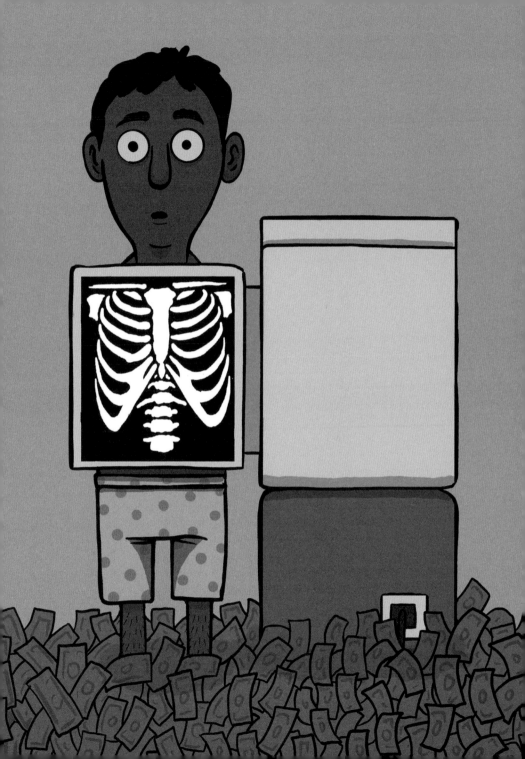

THERE WILL BE LOTS OF WAITING.

IN EVERY SOCIAL SITUATION
YOU'RE REPRESENTING MORE
THAN JUST YOURSELF.

YOU'LL PROBABLY FIND EVERYTHING
MORE EXPENSIVE.

YOU'RE GONNA BE BROKE. A LOT.

A JOB IS A JOB.

'SPICY' IS NOT SPICY.

NOT ALL BEARDS ARE
CREATED EQUAL.

PEOPLE WILL PUT YOU INTO A BOX...

...MAKE SURE YOU DON'T
JUMP INTO YOURS.

BE OPEN TO LEARNING ABOUT
OTHER CULTURES AS WELL AS
SHARING YOUR OWN.

PEOPLE ARE GONNA COMPLAIN
ABOUT THE PUBLIC TRANSPORT.

EVERYONE DRESSES ~~FUNNY~~
DIFFERENT.

SEASONS ARE STRANGE.

PEOPLE ARE GONNA GUESS
WHERE YOU'RE FROM. A LOT.

NOT EVERYONE IS GOING TO BE
HAPPY TO SEE YOU...

...SOME MAY LIKE YOU
A BIT TOO MUCH.

PEOPLE HERE REALLY, REALLY
LIKE THEIR PETS.

DEALING WITH THE POLICE IS
NERVE-WRACKING, NO MATTER
THE SITUATION.

SEASONS ARE STRANGE.

WHEN IT IS HOT, IT REALLY IS HOT!

IMITATION MIGHT NOT BE THE
SINCEREST FORM OF FLATTERY.

THE WORD 'AUTHENTIC' IS
THROWN AROUND A LOT.

THE BIGGER YOUR BANK ACCOUNT,
THE BETTER YOUR EDUCATION.

EVERYONE WANTS TO KNOW
WHAT VISA YOU'RE ON...

SEASONS ARE STRANGE.

YES, HOME IS FAR AWAY. BUT SO ARE
THE PRESSURES THAT COME WITH IT.

IT'S NORMAL TO LIVE WITH
STRANGERS — EVEN ENCOURAGED.

YOU'RE GONNA GET HOMESICK.

SOMETIMES YOU'RE GONNA NEED
TO STOP AND HAVE A GOOD LONG
LOOK AT YOURSELF...

...WHICH WILL LEAD TO MANY A SLEEPLESS NIGHT QUESTIONING HOW YOUR EXISTING VIEWS AND BELIEFS FIT INTO THIS NEW CULTURE.

YOU'RE GONNA HAVE TO THROW
AWAY STUFF YOU DON'T NEED...

...BUT BE CAREFUL NOT TO THROW EVERYTHING AWAY.

SEASONS ARE STRANGE.

NO MATTER WHAT YOU'RE
TALKING ABOUT - SOME PEOPLE
JUST WON'T LISTEN.

THERE IS PLENTY OF NEW LINGO
TO LEARN HERE.

PEOPLE SPEAK ENGLISH
DIFFERENTLY HERE.

CONTRADICTIONS ARE EVERYWHERE.

EQUALITY LOOKS DIFFERENT.

SOME PEOPLE FEEL LIKE THEY NEED
TO SPEAK ON YOUR BEHALF.

MORE PAPERWORK.

IT'S EASY TO FALL INTO THE TRAP OF
NURTURING THINGS THAT AREN'T
ACTUALLY GOOD FOR YOU.
EVEN IF YOU THINK THEY DEFINE YOU.

THE SPORT MIGHT CHANGE –
BUT THE FANS ARE THE SAME.

DON'T BE AFRAID TO TALK
ABOUT HOW YOU FEEL...

...IT'S ACTUALLY ENCOURAGED.

EVERYONE IS ON ANTIDEPRESSANTS.

EVERYTHING CAN BE COMMODIFIED.

THERE'S JUST TOILET PAPER.

THE NEWS WON'T ALWAYS BE KIND.

THE FEELING OF NOT BELONGING
MAY NEVER DISAPPEAR.

THE DISCOMFORT CAN GO
BOTH WAYS.

PEOPLE SEEM TO DISLIKE WALKING.

YOU'VE GOT FREEDOM OF SPEECH.*

*TERMS AND CONDITIONS APPLY

EVERYONE ALSO HAS THE
FREEDOM TO IGNORE YOU.

POLITICIANS ARE THE
SAME EVERYWHERE.

NOT EVERYONE WILL UNDERSTAND
WHAT YOU'VE BEEN THROUGH TO BE
WHERE YOU ARE NOW.

THE ELUSIVE CHASE.

YOU WON'T BE FORCED TO CHOOSE
BETWEEN FAMILY AND CAREER.

EVERYONE HAS BEEN TO OR WANTS
TO VISIT WHERE YOU'RE FROM.

FIRST GENERATION.

YOUR KIDS WON'T ALWAYS
UNDERSTAND OR APPRECIATE
WHAT IT TOOK TO MOVE HERE.

BE PATIENT.

ACHIEVEMENT-BASED AFFECTION ISN'T
A HEALTHY DYNAMIC IN ANY FAMILY.

BARS AND CAFES.
ANYWHERE AND EVERYWHERE.

JUST BECAUSE YOU DON'T LOOK
ALIKE DOESN'T MEAN THEY WON'T
HAVE YOUR BACK.

JUST BECAUSE YOU LOOK ALIKE
DOESN'T MEAN THEY HAVE
YOUR BACK.

IT'S NOT ALWAYS A COMPETITION.

IT'S EASY TO HATE, WHEN SOMEONE ELSE IS PULLING ALL THE STRINGS.

SURE, FLYING ECONOMY WAS
ANNOYING BUT NOT EVERYONE IS
THAT LUCKY.

CULTURAL STUDIES ARE AN ESSENTIAL PART OF INTERRACIAL RELATIONSHIPS.

FAMILY PHOTOGRAPHS
ARE A BIT DIFFERENT.

PIGEONS STILL WALK
FUNNY OVER HERE.

DID I MENTION PAPERWORK?

ACKNOWLEDGEMENTS

TO BE AN 'IMMIGRANT' ONE HAS TO LEAVE THEIR COUNTRY AND MAKE A HOME IN A FOREIGN COUNTRY. I WOULD LIKE TO USE THIS OPPORTUNITY TO ACKNOWLEDGE THE PEOPLE (AND BUNNY) WHO MADE THAT EXPERIENCE EASIER AND ALLOWED ME TO CREATE THIS BOOK.

FIRSTLY I'D LIKE TO THANK SARAH, FOR GIVING ME THE OPPORTUNITY TO STAY, FOR SUPPORTING ME THROUGH THE 'STAYING' AND FOR HELPING ME UNDERSTAND AND EXPERIENCE THINGS I MIGHT NOT HAVE ON MY OWN.

I'D LIKE TO THANK MY FAMILY AND EXTENDED FAMILY BACK HOME IN SRI LANKA, FOR ALL THE SACRIFICES YOU MADE TO HELP ME GET HERE, AND FOR THE EXPERIENCES I HAD GROWING UP THERE THAT ALLOWED ME TO HANDLE THE CHALLENGES I FACED ONCE I HAD LEFT.

I'D ALSO LIKE TO THANK BILL AND LORA, FOR BEING A
CONSTANT SOURCE OF SUPPORT AND ADVICE.

THERE IS A HUGE GAP BETWEEN HAVING AN IDEA AND
TURNING IT INTO A BOOK; I'D LIKE TO THANK MARTIN, THE
PUBLISHING DIRECTOR OF AFFIRM PRESS AND FELLOW
'WHISKEY' ENTHUSIAST FOR TAKING A CHANCE ON MY IDEA
AND FOR THE CONTINUOUS SUPPORT IN ALL MY PROJECTS.

I'D ALSO LIKE TO THANK THE REST OF THE TEAM AT AFFIRM
PRESS: STEPH, FREYA AND SASHA FOR HELPING ME THROUGH
THE PROCESS OF GETTING THIS BOOK PUBLISHED!

LAST BUT NOT LEAST, I'D LIKE TO THANK GRUMPY FOR BEING
A CONSTANT SOURCE OF INSPIRATION.

Published by Affirm Press in 2021
28 Thistlethwaite Street, South Melbourne, VIC 3205.
www.affirmpress.com.au
10 9 8 7 6 5 4 3 2 1

Title: What to Expect When You're Immigrating /
NASH, author–illustrator
ISBN: 9781925972894 (paperback)

A catalogue record for this
book is available from the
National Library of Australia

Cover and internal design by Affirm Press
Printed in China by C&C Offset Printing Co., Ltd.